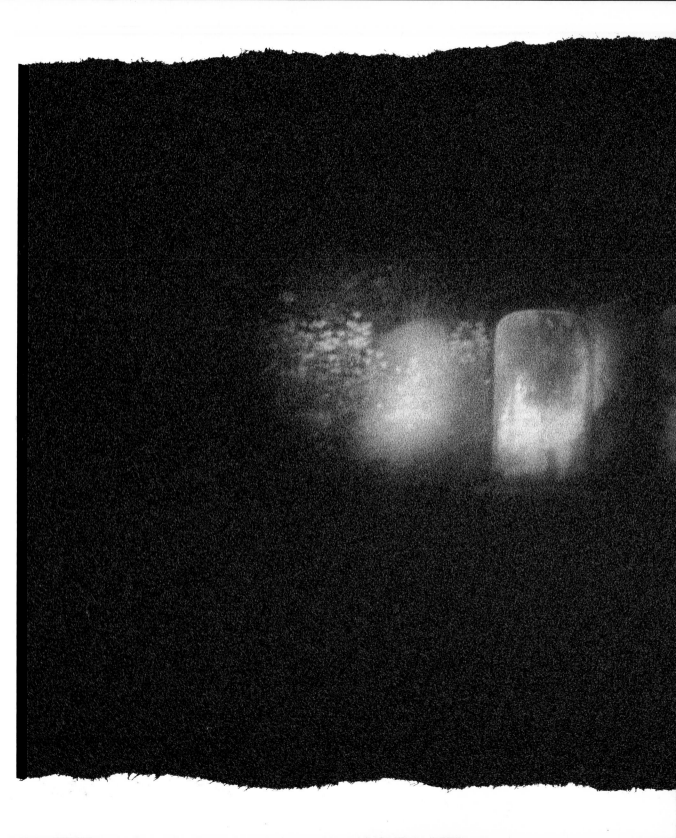

Text © 1993 Nancy Loewen
Photographs © 1993 Tina Mucci
Published in 1993 by Creative
Education, 123 South Broad Street,
Mankato, MN 56001 USA

Library of Congress Cataloging
Loewen, Nancy, Poe/Nancy Loewen.
Summary: Examines the life and
work of the nineteenth-century
author best known for his poetry and
stories of terror, grief, revenge, and
death. ISBN 0-88682-509-1
1. Poe, Edgar Allan, 1809–1849-
Juvenile literature. 2. Authors.
American—19th century—
Biography—Juvenile literature.
[1. Poe, Edgar Allan, 1809–1849.
2. Authors, American.] I. Title.
PS2631.L74   1992   92-3382
818'.309-dc20   CIP   [B]   AC

POE

A BIOGRAPHY

NANCY LOEWEN

PHOTOGRAPHIC
INTERPRETATION BY

TINA MUCCI

DESIGNED BY RITA MARSHALL

CREATIVE EDUCATION

For Bill
N.L.

For my mother
T.M.

It is a cold, windy night in 1845, but the people gathered in the parlor of a New York City home are warm and content. A fire is burning in the hearth. Lamps glow brightly throughout the room. A servant walks among the guests, offering coffee, tea, and brandy. The conversation is of telegraphs and President Polk and the annexation of Texas. Suddenly one voice rises above the chatter. "Mr. Poe!" implores a young woman. "We would be so honored if you would recite 'The Raven' to us this evening."

A murmur of agreement spreads through the room as everyone turns toward the small, dark-haired man sitting in a corner chair. A look of arrogant satisfaction crosses his face. Then he smiles and jumps nimbly to his

feet. "Certainly," he says, moving to the center of the room. "But I would really prefer that the lights be dimmed."

The host and hostess quickly rise to comply with Edgar Allan Poe's request. With the lights dimmed, the room seems colder; the wind outside, more desperate.

Poe stands before the group, waiting for just the right moment to begin. He is thin and pale; his clothes are well worn and slightly out of style. But no one thinks twice about those things. What impresses them instead is his confident manner and the shiny intensity of his large eyes.

At last Poe breathes deeply and begins his recitation. His voice is low and smooth as he half speaks, half sings the eerie lines.

Once upon a midnight dreary, while I pondered, weak and weary,

Over many a quaint and curious volume of forgotten lore—

While I nodded, nearly napping, suddenly there came a tapping,

As of some one gently rapping, rapping at my chamber door—

"'Tis some visitor," I muttered, "tapping at my chamber door—

Only this and nothing more."

The poem tells the story of a man who is mourning the death of the woman he loved. As he sits in his study on a windy night, he is startled by a noise outside his window. He opens the shutters— and a large black raven swoops into the room. The raven can speak, but it knows just one word: NEVERMORE. To the grieving man, the raven and its message are unbearable reminders of the finality of death.

As Poe continues, stanza after stanza, the people before him are drawn into the strange horror and sadness of the poem. One man glances nervously at the window beside him, as if expecting to see the black flapping wings of the raven. A few of the women listen with their eyes closed, folding their hands tightly in their laps. Others, clutching their cups of tea or glasses of brandy, keep a wary eye on the shadows flickering against the wall.

Poe himself seems to be in another world. His voice rises passionately.

"PROPHET!" SAID I, "THING OF EVIL!—PROPHET STILL, IF BIRD OR DEVIL!

BY THAT HEAVEN THAT BENDS ABOVE US—BY THAT GOD WE BOTH ADORE—

TELL THIS SOUL WITH SORROW LADEN IF, WITHIN THE DISTANT AIDENN,

IT SHALL CLASP A SAINTED MAIDEN WHOM THE ANGELS NAME LENORE—

CLASP A RARE AND RADIANT MAIDEN WHOM THE ANGELS NAME LENORE."

QUOTH THE RAVEN "NEVERMORE."

The small audience hardly breathes as the hypnotic rhythm of the poem flows through the room. With a wild gleam in his eye, Poe recites the final stanza.

And the Raven, never flitting, still is sitting, *STILL* is sitting

On the pallid bust of Pallas just above my chamber door;

And his eyes have all the seeming of a demon's that is dreaming,

And the lamp-light o'er him streaming throws his shadow on the floor;

And my soul from out that shadow that lies floating on the floor

Shall be lifted—nevermore!

Like the raven in his poem, Edgar Allan Poe's voice still haunts the world. He is best known for his stories of terror, grief, revenge, and death, and for his poetry. But Poe's contribution to literature goes beyond that. His love of reason, of the logical process that allows one to solve a difficult puzzle, led him to write the first detective stories. He is also known for his work as a literary critic and theorist. At a time when American culture was still very much influenced by Great Britain, Poe was a powerful force on the literary scene—nagging and boasting, criticizing and satirizing, pleading and praising. His efforts won him more enemies than friends, but in the end he helped shape American literature in his own time and beyond.

Poe was a master at creating a single, unified effect in his work. "All his ideas, like obedient arrows, fly to the same target," observed the French writer Charles-Pierre Baudelaire.

Unfortunately, the same might be said about his life. His mother died before he was three years old; his foster mother before he was twenty. His wife died at the age of twenty-four after suffering from tuberculosis for five years. He had a troubled relationship with his foster father, and his poverty and alcoholism were burdens he was never able to overcome. And always, always in the back of his mind was the fear that he was losing his sanity.

The story of his life is nearly as compelling, and as horrifying, as the tales that sprang from his dark imagination.

ONE

I am the descendant of a race whose imaginative and easily excitable temperament has at all times rendered them remarkable; and, in my earliest infancy, I gave evidence of having fully inherited the family character. As I advanced in years it was more strongly developed; becoming, for many reasons, a cause of serious disquietude to my friends, and of positive injury to myself. I grew self-willed, addicted to the wildest caprices, and a prey to the most ungovernable passions.

FROM "WILLIAM WILSON"

Although Poe wasn't referring directly to himself in these lines, his perception of himself may well have been similar. Edgar Allan Poe's parents were actors. His mother, Elizabeth Arnold, was a dark-haired beauty and the main attraction of the acting company in which she worked; his father, David Poe, Jr., was a handsome but reckless man with a never-ending compulsion to drink. They were married in 1806 and had their first child, William Henry, in 1807. Their second son was born in Boston on January 19, 1809, while the acting company was performing Shakespeare's *Hamlet.* Elizabeth named him Edgar, after a theater manager who had been kind to her. When Edgar was still a baby, David Poe mysteriously deserted his family, leaving Elizabeth—who was pregnant again—to care for their children. This was a daunting task. Most actors in those days were very poor and spent their lives traveling in drafty coaches from one city to the next. Elizabeth struggled to support her children, but the effort soon wore down her strength.

After her daughter Rosalie was

born, Elizabeth sent young William Henry to live with David Poe's family in Baltimore, hoping for the day when they could all be together again. She soon realized that day would never come. Frail and exhausted, Elizabeth Poe developed tuberculosis, a disease of the lungs that was often called consumption. It was a death sentence. She grew weaker and weaker, and on December 8, 1811, Elizabeth Poe died in Richmond, Virginia, at the age of twenty-four.

Edgar Poe and his baby sister were then separated from each

other, although both stayed in Richmond. Rosalie was taken in by a family named MacKenzie. Edgar, not quite three years old, was sent to live in the home of Frances and John Allan. John Allan was a general merchant and tobacco exporter. The couple had no children of their own.

Edgar Poe's early years with the Allan family were pleasant. He might have missed the smell of stage makeup and the rustle of costumes that he associated with his mother, but those memories faded and he was soon calling Frances "Ma." Frances and her sister, who also lived with the family, praised and pampered Edgar. Even the business-minded John Allan would set aside his ledgers and permit himself to smile as he watched Edgar recite verses, or dance on the dining room table in his stocking feet.

When Edgar was six years old, his world suddenly changed again: John Allan took his family with him on an extended business trip to England. They would be gone five years.

Although Edgar was very young when his family moved to England, his experiences during those years would later have a great influence on his work. The journey itself—thirty-four days aboard a ship on the Atlantic Ocean, surrounded by endless sky and water and wind—was thrilling to the adventurous child. In a letter to his business partner, John Allan wrote, "Edgar says say something for me Pa say I was not afraid coming across the Sea."

For a year Edgar traveled about the country with his foster parents, but the time soon came for his education to begin. He attended a London academy in 1816, and in the fall of the following year he went to the Manor House School in Stoke Newington. This was a boarding school near London, and with its ancient, gloomy buildings, elm-lined paths, and faraway hills, it was very different from anything Edgar had experienced before.

The schoolroom was long and narrow, with an oak-lined ceiling and windows that let in a musty light. The playground was filled with gravel and surrounded by a spiked, iron-studded gate. The bedroom where he studied and slept and, perhaps, tentatively began to write was small and sparsely furnished; to reach it he had to pass through a maze of narrow halls and dimly lit staircases. Standing outside the building, try as he might, he couldn't tell which small window belonged to his room.

Judging from the tales and poems he would later write, the three years Edgar Allan Poe spent at the Manor House School were important ones. He seemed to absorb the Gothic atmosphere into his very soul.

T W O

A fifteen-year-old boy passes through the gate of a Richmond cemetery. As he walks down the path, his strides are purposeful, his shoulders set back confidently. But as he draws closer to a certain freshly dug grave, his steps grow shaky and his shoulders slump. He stumbles to the foot of the grave and, kneeling in the dirt, begins to cry.

"My beautiful Helen," he says when he is able to. "How can it be that you are dead?"

But he is answered only with silence, a heavy, eternal silence that rings in his ears and causes him to grind his teeth in anguish.

Nearby, the cemetery caretaker and his wife are passing by on another path. Through the trees they see the weeping figure of the boy; they watch as he shakes his fists at the cloudy springtime sky.

"Who's that?" the caretaker's wife asks suspiciously. "What's the matter with him?"

The caretaker shrugs. "Oh, that's just Edgar Poe, John Allan's ward. He's here nearly every day. I don't know why he's so upset—Jane Stanard was just the mother of a classmate of his. She went insane, I hear."

The caretaker's wife glances once more at the boy and keeps on walking. And after a while, Edgar Allan Poe stands up, brushes the dirt off his clothes, and goes home.

The image of a beautiful dying woman occurred often in Poe's work, and in his life as well. As a young child he had watched the feverish face of his mother while she slowly died. Now, at the age of fifteen, he once again experienced the loss of a woman who was important to him. Jane Stanard was the young mother of Edgar's classmate, Robert, and Edgar had a curious sort of crush on her. Mrs. Stanard was kind and gracious, and she seemed to listen to him with a respect he couldn't get at home or at school. And she was so

beautiful! He always referred to her as "Helen," a name that, in classical literature, is often associated with beauty.

The comfort Edgar received from spending time in Jane Stanard's presence was short-lived. She became ill and died in April 1824. Edgar was just beginning to realize the power of his imagination, and for a time he let his grief consume him.

Painful as this loss was, it eventually led to the creation of one of Poe's best-loved poems, "To Helen," and to one of poetry's most celebrated stanzas:

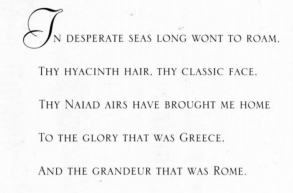

*I*n desperate seas long wont to roam,

Thy hyacinth hair, thy classic face,

Thy Naiad airs have brought me home

To the glory that was Greece,

And the grandeur that was Rome.

Edgar's obsession with Jane Stanard set him apart from his peers, yet in other ways his adolescence was completely normal. The Allan family had returned to Richmond when Edgar was eleven years old, and in the years that followed Edgar was busy with school and sports. He liked running and boxing and was a particularly strong swimmer. He once swam the James River from Ludlam's Wharf to Warwick, a distance of six miles.

In school, Edgar was known for his good grades, which he managed to get without studying very much. Most of the time he got along well with his classmates, but when he disagreed with someone, he could be very stubborn—not to mention sharp-tongued. And he never asked anyone to come home with him at the end of the school day.

When Edgar had attended school in England, he had been a bit of an outsider and was probably the only student who spoke with a southern accent. Now, back in Richmond, he still had the feeling that he didn't quite fit in. During the years he'd been away, his classmates had grown up together and established friendships. Besides, everyone knew that his real parents had been actors—a disreputable profession in those days—and that the Allans had never legally adopted him.

"All this had the effect of making the boys decline his leadership," a classmate commented years later. "On looking back on it since, I fancy it gave him a fierceness he would otherwise not have had."

If Edgar Poe was "fierce" at school, he was even more so at home. Although he treated Frances Allan with consideration and love, he frequently argued with his foster father. John Allan seemed to expect constant, humble gratitude for having taken Edgar in as a child, but that sort of humility just wasn't in Edgar's nature. The more Allan criticized him, the more defiant Edgar became.

The ill will between them grew deeper in the fall of 1824, when Edgar made the startling discovery that John Allan had been seeing other women. To an idealistic teenager who adored his foster mother, this behavior was unforgivable. Edgar became

increasingly unpleasant to live with, and before long he and John Allan could hardly stand to be in the same room with each other.

The tension in the household was somewhat relieved in March 1825, when John Allan inherited a fortune from a wealthy uncle. The Allans had never been poor, but they had never been rich, either—until now. They soon bought a house in a fashionable neighborhood and began enjoying their new prestige.

At this time Edgar was probably studying with a private tutor, preparing for his entrance to the University of Virginia. He liked his academic work, and he thought it was interesting to talk to the well-educated people who were guests at the Allans' new home. But something even more exciting was taking place: Edgar Poe was secretly engaged to a neighbor girl, Sarah Elmira Royster.

In Sarah's eyes, Edgar was handsome and elegant, a true gentleman. "Edgar was a beautiful

boy; he was not very talkative, and his general manner was sad, but when he did talk his conversation was very pleasant," Sarah later recalled. "Edgar was warm and zealous in any cause he was interested in, being enthusiastic and impulsive. He had strong prejudices, and hated everything coarse and unrefined."

John Allan, however, hadn't changed his opinion of his foster son; he wanted the boy out of his sight, and sending him to the University of Virginia seemed like the perfect plan.

THREE

Edgar Allan Poe stands before the fireplace in his room at the University of Virginia, reading his latest story to a few of his friends. They listen, spellbound, as his impassioned voice rises and falls with the action of the story. At last he finishes and looks at them expectantly.

Edgar's friends admire his work and have often told him so. But tonight they're not in the mood for a serious literary discussion. They tease Poe instead.

"There's just one thing wrong with it, Edgar," announces one of the students. "The hero's name —Gaffy—comes up too often."

The others are quick to catch on. "That's right," another student nods. "Get rid of the 'Gaffies' and you'll have quite a piece there, I'd say!"

Edgar stands very still as he listens to his friends make fun of his story. He knows they're just kidding around, and he knows he is a gifted writer, but he can't seem to stop the rage that is

building up inside him. Suddenly, without thinking about what he is doing, he flings the entire manuscript into the fire.

"Wait! No! Don't do that!" his friends exclaim in alarm, but Edgar merely turns his back to them as the pages burn. The students file out of the room, bewildered by Edgar's violent reaction.

The next day Edgar apologizes to his friends for the incident. And from then on, whenever they want to tease Edgar, they call him Gaffy. Edgar scowls a little every time he hears the name, but he's too embarrassed to say anything.

Edgar Allan Poe arrived in Charlottesville in February 1826, eager to begin his college education. At that time the University of Virginia, founded by Thomas Jefferson, had been open for just one term. The professors were distinguished scholars, many of them from Europe. The students were part of an experiment that the nation's educators were watching carefully: They were to be self-governing.

Edgar thrived in the unrestrictive university atmosphere, but something was bothering him. He hadn't received one letter from Sarah, even though he'd written many letters to her. Besides that, he was always short of money.

John Allan had sent Edgar off to school with too little money to pay his bills. Again and again, Edgar wrote to his foster father and begged for more money, but Allan had long ago turned a deaf ear to Edgar's concerns.

Most of Edgar's fellow students —177 young men from thirteen states—were the sons of wealthy southern planters and spent money without a second thought. They drank, gambled, hired servants, bought fine clothes, and indulged in all sorts of amusements. Edgar, on the other hand, had to buy his books on credit. He had to drop one of his classes because he didn't have money for tuition.

As the term continued, Edgar grew desperate. He took to gambling to try to increase his funds. But he kept losing, and as his debt got out of hand, so did his drinking. "He played in so impassioned a manner that it amounted almost to infatuation," a friend from that time observed. "Card-playing and drinking alike were carried on under the spell of impulse or uncontrolled excitement."

As misguided as Edgar's actions were, he was hardly alone. The experiment with student self-government was failing. In fact, gambling had become such a problem that local authorities were forced to intervene. One morning the sheriff and his officers appeared on campus, ready to arrest the students who were known to be the worst gamblers. But the young men ran off to the woods and hid in a secluded spot Edgar had discovered on one of his walks. They stayed there for several days—playing cards to while away the hours!

The students might have gambled for fun, but their debts were taken seriously. By December, the end of his first and only term at the university, Edgar owed more than two thousand dollars to various people. John Allan refused to pay those debts, even though he was partly responsible for the situation, and he didn't allow Edgar to return to the school. Edgar's college career was over.

His romance with Sarah Elmira Royster was over as well. When Edgar came back to Richmond, he discovered that Sarah was about to marry another man. The truth came out too late: Her father had been intercepting their letters. Sarah, thinking Edgar had forgotten about her, had agreed to marry a man who had her parents' approval.

For three months after he left the University of Virginia, Poe remained in Richmond, wearily putting up with John Allan's criticism. Then, in March 1827, he left home abruptly after yet another quarrel with his foster father.

"My determination is at length taken to leave your house and to endeavor to find some place in this world, where I will be treated —not as you have treated me," Poe announced bitterly in a letter to Allan. But he was still dependent on Allan, as he well knew—

and that fact must have infuriated him. The letter closed in a vaguely threatening tone: "Send me I entreat you some money immediately, as I am in the greatest necessity. If you fail to comply with my request—I tremble for the consequences."

Using a false name, Poe booked passage on a coal ship to Boston, the city where he was born. There is some evidence that he tried to make a go of acting, as his parents did. Nothing came of

that, but while in Boston Poe did manage to publish his first book. *Tamerlane and Other Poems* was published in the summer of 1827 by Calvin Thomas, a printer who, at nineteen, was just a year older than Poe. Only forty copies of the book were printed, each copy selling for twelve and a half cents. The book was signed by "a Bostonian," Poe's ploy to attract more attention in the sophisticated literary circles of Boston. It didn't work.

By the time the book came out, however, Poe had already gone ahead with other plans. With little money and few friends, he enlisted in the U.S. Army on May 26, 1827, using the name Edgar A. Perry. He lied about his age, saying he was twenty-two when he was actually just eighteen.

It seems odd that a troubled young writer would choose to live in a disciplined military environment, but "Edgar A. Perry" did quite well. The structure and rou-

tine appealed to him at that point in his life, and within a year and a half he achieved the rank of sergeant major, the highest rank a noncommissioned officer could obtain.

But Poe was starting to feel restless. He thought that if he could get an appointment to the West Point military academy, he could become a military officer and make a better career for himself. In order to get an honorable discharge from the army, however, Poe needed John Allan's permission to leave.

At that time, Frances Allan was very ill, but she was concerned about Poe's future. On her deathbed, she pleaded with her husband to help the young man. Although his heart wasn't in it, Allan promised his dying wife that he would do what he could to assist Poe's career.

Allan kept his word. When Frances died on February 28, 1829, he helped Poe arrange for a leave and sent him money for the trip home to Richmond. Poe arrived the day after the burial, distraught with grief over his foster mother's death but hopeful that he and John Allan would finally be able to put their differences behind them.

And for a time it seemed that they would. Allan gave Poe written permission to leave the army, and, as was the custom then, paid for a substitute to take Poe's place. On April 15, 1829, Edgar Allan Poe was given an honorable discharge from the army, and he soon made his application to West Point.

More than a year passed before Poe actually entered West Point, and he made use of his time. During a long visit to Baltimore he published his second volume of poems, *Al Aaraaf, Tamerlane, and Minor Poems.* Poe apparently still thought of himself as a poet, despite his plans for a military career. In a letter to a potential publisher he wrote: "I am young —not yet twenty—*am* a poet—if deep worship of all beauty can make me one—and wish to be so in the more common meaning of the word. I would give the world to embody one half the ideas afloat in my imagination."

While in Baltimore, Poe finally met his real father's family. His grandfather had died, but he soon got to know his other relatives, including his father's kindhearted, practical sister, Maria Clemm, and her young daughter, Virginia— who, just six years later, would become his wife.

F O U R

It's a rainy November night at West Point, in the year 1830. Edgar Allan Poe sneaks out of his barracks and stands under a tree, watching carefully for signs of trouble. At last his roommate T. H. Gibson darts through the rain and joins him, clutching a bottle of brandy and a recently slaughtered goose.

"I got the stuff!" Gibson exclaims breathlessly. "Old Benny wouldn't give me a chicken, but he let me have this

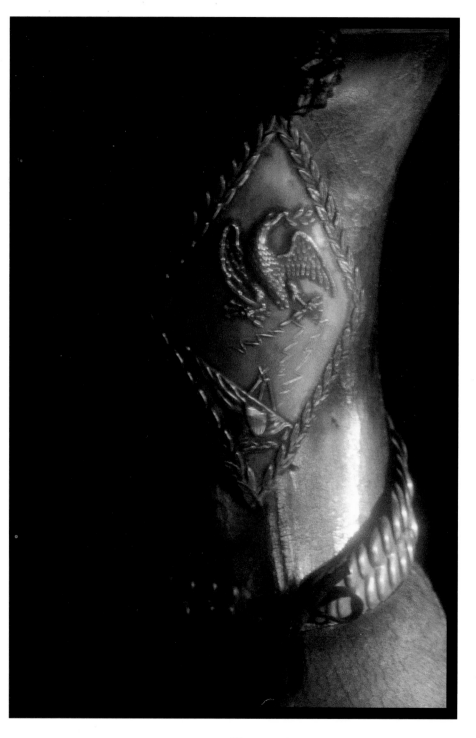

goose. It'll make a good supper, don't you think? And won't this brandy sweeten up the night!"

Poe looks at his friend, whose face and clothes are splotched with blood from the goose. He thinks of his other roommate, who is waiting for them back in the room, along with a friend. Suddenly he laughs. "I have an idea about how we can scare the others," he says. "Here's the plan. . . ."

Fifteen minutes later, Poe, his roommate, and a fellow cadet are studying in their room when Gibson staggers drunkenly through the door. His face and clothes are smeared with blood. "My God!" Poe exclaims, pretending to be startled. "What happened to you?"

The other two cadets stare in horror as Gibson stumbles around the room, waving a bloodstained knife and muttering the name of his professor. "I killed him!" he cries.

"This is just a joke," Poe protests, but Gibson shakes his head violently and steps back toward the door. "Here's the

proof. I cut off his head!" And with that Gibson grabs the goose and swings it into the room, knocking over the only lit candle. The cadets get a split-second glimpse of the unidentifiable mass —and then the room goes dark.

The visiting cadet screams and escapes through the window. He races back to his own barracks, yelling at the top of his lungs that Gibson has killed a professor. The other cadet, the roommate, trembles in the corner.

Poe and Gibson relight the candle and, laughing uncontrolla-

bly, reassure their bewildered roommate that no murder has taken place. Then they pour themselves some brandy and congratulate themselves on their best prank yet.

Like most of his fellow cadets at West Point, Edgar Allan Poe managed to amuse himself despite the academy's many rules and regulations. Besides masterminding the occasional prank, he delighted his peers by writing sarcastic, witty verses about the instructors. And, as usual, he did well in his classes. In fact, it was rumored that he never spent more than two minutes preparing his lessons.

But Poe was never a typical cadet. By this time his health had begun to fail, and he looked much older than he actually was. One of his friends described him as having a "worn, weary, discontented look."

From Poe's point of view, he had plenty to be discontented about. Most of the cadets received allowances from home, but John Allan didn't send any money; as a result, Poe was embarrassingly poor, as usual. Furthermore, Allan had remarried, which seriously hurt Poe's chances of ever inheriting anything from him.

When Poe entered West Point, he thought that he would be able to breeze through the course work and become an officer in a matter of months. This was not the case, as he soon discovered. The idea of a career as a military officer quickly lost its appeal. In a calculated effort, Poe neglected his classes and other duties and was promptly dismissed from the academy.

⸺

When Poe left West Point in February 1831, he headed for New York City, where he hoped to make his dreams of greatness come true. But the twenty-two-year-old became ill instead, suffering from a painful ear infection and a recurring state of depression. He began taking opium to escape from the pain and from the terrors of his imagination. The drug only made his nightmares more vivid, however, and he soon gave it up.

One good thing did come of his stay in New York. His third book of poetry, *Poems by Edgar A. Poe, Second Edition,* was published. The book contained several poems that are among Poe's best-known works today, including "To Helen," "Israfel," and "The City in the Sea." It was dedicated to his fellow cadets at West Point, many of whom had paid for it in advance. When the book finally came out, though, the cadets felt cheated. They'd been expecting a book of Poe's funny, sarcastic verses—not, as one cadet put it, "ridiculous doggerel" poetry.

Lonely and discouraged, Poe next went to Baltimore, where he lived with his relatives. The household was made up of his grandmother; his older brother, William Henry, who died of tuberculosis and alcoholism shortly after Poe moved in; his aunt, Maria Clemm; and his two cousins, Virginia and Henry. Although Poe found companionship with them, it seemed his problems were just beginning. The only steady income in the family was a small pension paid to Poe's grandmother. Edgar tried to get a job as a teacher or a newspaper reporter, but his efforts didn't lead to anything permanent.

Disheartened by the lack of response to his poetry, Poe began writing short stories. In 1832 the *Philadelphia Saturday Courier* published five of his stories, and the following year Poe won first prize—and a badly needed fifty dollars—in a contest sponsored by the *Baltimore Saturday Visitor.* The winning story, "MS Found in a Bottle," was a nightmarish tale about a phantom ship.

Although he was far removed from his past life in Richmond, Poe had not completely broken with his foster father. Since leaving West Point, he had occasionally written to John Allan, begging for money and issuing vague threats. One let-

ter, however, revealed a different attitude. On October 16, 1831, Poe wrote: "It is a long time since I have written to you unless with an application for money or assistance. I am sorry that it is so seldom that I hear from you or even of you—for all communication seems to be at an end; and when I think of the long twenty-one years that I have called you father, and you have called me son, I could cry like a child to think that it should all end in this."

But Poe and John Allan were never reconciled. One story is that shortly before Allan's death, Poe visited him in Richmond; supposedly Edgar pushed aside Allan's second wife and went into the bedroom, where a startled John Allan threatened to hit him with his cane if Edgar came any closer.

Whether that happened or not, it is true that John Allan had completely washed his hands of his foster son. That became perfectly clear after Allan's death on March 27, 1834. In his will, Allan provided generously for his second wife and their three children, and for his illegitimate children as well. For Edgar, the orphan, there was nothing.

ℱIVE

And then came, as if to my final and irrevocable overthrow, the spirit of PERVERSENESS. *Of this spirit philosophy takes no account. Yet I am not more sure that my soul lives, than I am that perverseness is one of the primitive impulses of the human heart—one of the indivisible primary faculties, or sentiments, which give direction to the character of Man. Who has not, a hundred times, found himself committing a vile or silly action, for no other reason than because he knows he should* not*? Have we*

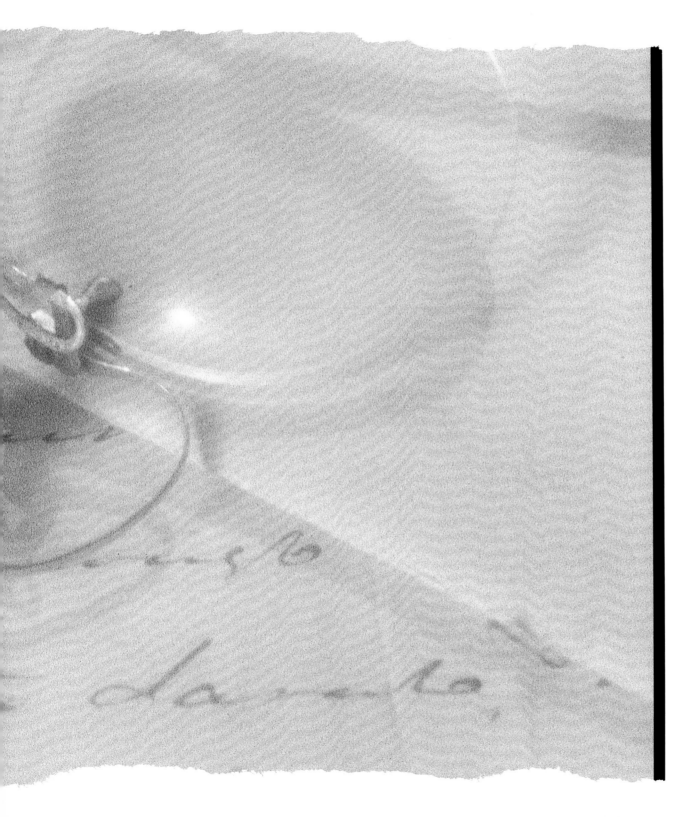

not a perpetual inclination, in the
teeth of our best judgment, to vio-
late that which is <u>*Law*</u>*, merely*
because we understand it to be
such? This spirit of perverseness,
I say, came to my final overthrow.

FROM "THE BLACK CAT"

*E*dgar Allan Poe was already
well acquainted with "the spirit of
perverseness." He'd gambled his
way out of a university education
and thrown away his chances for a
military career. Now he stood at
the brink of literary success, but
despite his enormous talent, he
would never quite manage to dig
in his heels and make a stable life

for himself. No matter how hard he tried, the time would eventually come when he did the very things he knew he should not—quarrel with his bosses, infuriate fellow writers, go on drunken sprees that left his health in a shambles and his heart ashamed. The pattern had already been set.

In the summer of 1835, Poe was offered a position as an assistant editor at the *Southern Literary Messenger*. He took the job, even though it meant moving back to Richmond. Oddly enough, his office was right next to the storefront of John Allan's old business.

But Poe put that phase of his life behind him as he industriously wrote stories, reviews, and literary notices for the *Messenger*. He soon made a name for himself, particularly for his reviews. He had no tolerance for mediocre writers, and the circulation of the *Messenger* shot up—from five hundred to more than thirty-five hundred—as more and more people sought out his intelligent and delightfully nasty reviews.

Poe was finally beginning to establish the literary career he'd longed for, but he still suffered from bouts of loneliness and

depression. He began drinking again, which, despite his success, put his job in jeopardy.

In this desperate state of mind, Poe clung to the only family he had left: Maria Clemm and Virginia. He was worried about them. His grandmother had died recently, and without her pension he didn't know how they would survive. Poe himself was struggling to make ends meet, yet he sent them a little money whenever he could.

Poe's concern for their well-being went beyond family duty, however. He intended to marry

his cousin Virginia. That fall, at Poe's insistent invitation, Virginia and her mother moved to Richmond, and the following spring, on May 16, 1836, Edgar and Virginia were married. Virginia was not quite fourteen years old.

People have suggested all sorts of theories to explain Poe's unusual marriage. Some think that Poe wanted to marry Virginia just to keep Maria Clemm near him, because of the motherly comfort she provided. Others believe that the couple never had a real marriage, but treated each other like brother and sister. In fact, Edgar

often called Virginia Sis or Sissy.

As unusual as their marriage was, though, it worked for them. Virginia *was* young when she married her "cousin Eddy," but as she grew up her devotion to him —and his to her—only became stronger. Virginia was sweet and smart and had a way of making others feel welcome and at ease. And she was always willing to learn new things, which made her a pleasant companion for Poe.

In the Allan household, Poe had often felt like an outsider, criticized for everything he did. Now, with Virginia and her mother, he had a family of his own—people who loved him unconditionally and who never uttered a critical word against him. Maybe now he would be able to keep those demons, those thoughts of despair and lunacy, at bay.

After a year and a half with the *Southern Literary Messenger,* and living in near poverty despite his hard work, Poe decided to try his luck in New York once again. Maria and Virginia kept a boardinghouse there, while Poe continued to write and look for full-time work. In July 1838 he published his only book-length story, *The Narrative of Arthur Gordon Pym,* which told the story of a horrifying and incredible shipwreck. In the introduction he claimed that he, Edgar A. Poe, had been told the story by a sailor who had actually been on the voyage. That, and the story's realistic details, fooled many people—including some reviewers— into believing the events had actually happened.

About the time the book came out, Poe and his family moved again, this time to Philadelphia. During their six-year stay there, Poe worked for two magazines, *Burton's Gentlemen's Magazine* and *Graham's Magazine.* He was entering his most productive period as a writer and critic and was back in form with his bold, arrogant reviews. He once referred to some of James Fenimore Cooper's books as "a flashy succession of ill-conceived and miserably executed literary productions, each more silly than its predecessor." No wonder Poe sometimes had trouble getting along with other writers!

In 1840 Poe published *Tales of the Grotesque and Arabesque,* a two-volume collection containing twenty-five stories—everything he'd written up to that time. One of the tales was called "The Fall of the House of Usher." In the story, Roderick Usher's beloved twin sister dies, and he locks up her coffin in the deep, tomblike cellar of his house. As the tale progresses, Usher and the friend who helped him bury his sister hear strange noises coming from beneath the house. In one hideous moment, days later, they realize what they have done: *"We have put her living in the tomb!"*

Like most of Poe's stories, "The Fall of the House of Usher" can be interpreted symbolically. Roderick Usher, his twin sister, and even the decaying building they live in can be thought of as different parts of the human psyche. Much of Poe's work deals with the question of identity, and with internal conflict. For example, "William Wilson," also written during this period, tells of a man who is haunted by a person who looks exactly like him. The man finally kills his double—his conscience—only to be destroyed himself. That Poe's stories can be interpreted on several levels is one of the reasons his work is still popular today.

No matter how strange or tortured his stories were, Poe's home life remained peaceful. Visitors often commented on the refined atmosphere of Poe's household, and despite their poverty, Edgar, Virginia, and Maria Clemm remained absolutely devoted to one another.

Poe's domestic happiness, however, was doomed to end. In January 1842, while preparing to sing for dinner guests, Virginia coughed up blood—an unmistakable sign of tuberculosis.

Poe later wrote: "Her life was despaired of. I took leave of her forever and underwent all the agonies of her death. She recovered partially and again I hoped. At the end of a year the vessel broke again. . . . Then again —again—again and even once again . . . I became insane, with long intervals of horrible sanity. During these fits of absolute consciousness I drank, God only knows how often or how much."

But Poe did more than drink during this period; he wrote like a man possessed. The frustration and horror he was experiencing poured out of his pen into some of literature's most intense and terrifying stories. "The Tell-Tale Heart" and "The Black Cat" are chilling tales of murder and insanity. "The Pit and the Pendulum" tells of a war prisoner who is tortured by a slowly descending pendulum that is meant to kill him.

Poe's story "The Gold Bug" was the most popular one during his lifetime. It tells of a man who discovers buried treasure by breaking a mysterious code. Poe had long had an interest in cryptography—the science of making and breaking codes—and had once written a newspaper column

in which he solved coded messages sent to him by readers. He was not quite the expert he pretended to be, but he presented his ideas with such authority that readers never questioned him.

In 1841 Poe wrote what is considered to be the first detective story, "The Murders in the Rue Morgue." Using the same main character, C. Auguste Dupin, Poe wrote "The Mystery of Marie Roget" in 1843 and "The Purloined Letter" two years later. Perhaps the world of logic offered Poe some relief from the constant anguish of Virginia's illness.

Poe and his family moved back to New York City in 1844. Less than a year later, in January 1845, Poe published the poem that, according to his contemporaries, established him once and for all as a major American writer. "The Raven" appeared in the *Evening Mirror,* on which Poe worked as an assistant editor. It was soon reprinted in many other publications. With its surreal images and strange, droning beauty, the poem captured the attention of people in both the United States and Europe. There was even talk of replacing the bald eagle with the raven as the national bird.

Poe was pleased with his new fame, but he had not yet realized his most cherished goal: to own and edit his own journal. He envisioned a thick, classy, expensive publication that contained only the best literature America had to offer. In the past, even when working for other magazines, he had clung to his dream and had even publicly announced his intention to launch a magazine "where may be found at all times, and upon all subjects, an honest and fearless opinion."

For a brief time Poe did get a taste of what it was like to own his own publication, but for him, that taste was bitter. The *Broadway Journal* was already in financial trouble when he started working there as an editor in the spring of 1845. Nevertheless, that fall Poe bought out the previous owner's interest for just fifty dollars. He spent much of his time trying to borrow money to keep the magazine going. Nothing could save it, however, and the magazine ceased publication in January 1846.

By now Poe had published three more books: *The Prose Romances of Edgar A. Poe, Tales by Edgar A. Poe,* and *The Raven and Other Poems.* The books were well received, but they didn't bring in much money—a fact that continually frustrated him as he struggled to support his family.

That summer Poe, his wife, and his mother-in-law moved to a small cottage in the country. Exhausted from his failed venture and from the fits of drinking and depression it caused, he was ill for a long time and unable to work. And Virginia had reached the final stages of her illness.

S I X

Virginia Poe lies on a cheap straw mattress in her bedroom. She is wrapped in her husband's overcoat and clean white sheets. Edgar sits next to her, holding her hands to keep them warm; her mother does the same with her feet. A brown tabby cat is curled warmly on her chest. "Catterina knows just what to do," Edgar comments softly, referring to the cat. "How Catterina loves you, Virginia!" Virginia says nothing, but for a moment her fever-glazed eyes

seem to hold a smile. Edgar continues to talk to her in a calm, soothing voice; he strokes her hair and presses her hand to his cheek. Her mother fusses with the sheets, tucking them closer to her body, and sits down again.

As the minutes tick away, Edgar tries to keep love and strength in his eyes. But every time Virginia coughs, every time she trembles, Edgar's own body shivers in an uncontrollable response.

It is in those moments that the love in his eyes is replaced with terror. Images of the inevitable flash in his mind—of Virginia's last breath, of her cold flesh and unseeing eyes, of her body being lowered into the earth. He longs to die with her, or to die in her place; he longs for her to die soon and bring an end to this torment. He struggles to keep himself from groaning out loud.

But in a few moments, when Virginia's frightened eyes again meet his, Edgar's face expresses only tenderness.

"Let me tell you about something funny that happened to me today," he says, and continues to hold his dying wife's hands.

On January 30, 1847, Virginia Poe died of tuberculosis at the age of twenty-four. She was buried in a nearby vault that belonged to the owners of the country cottage where they were staying. For weeks Poe got up in the middle of the night, weeping bitterly, and wandered out to his wife's grave. The only way he could sleep was if Maria Clemm, or some other woman, sat by his side and gently stroked his brow.

Gradually Poe recovered enough to write again. Often, as he bent over his manuscripts, Catterina sat across his shoulders and purred.

In *Eureka,* a book-length prose poem, Poe discussed his ideas about the nature of the universe, covering topics such as space, matter, time, and his conception of God. He also began concentrating on his poetry again. "The Bells," a poem of strong emotions and rich and varied sounds, was written during this time, as was the dark and melancholy "Ulalume."

But Poe had entered a downward cycle after Virginia's death, and it was one from which he would never emerge. As one

acquaintance observed, "The loss of his wife was a sad blow to him. He did not seem to care, after she was gone, whether he lived an hour, a day, a week, or a year."

Despite his melancholy, Poe hadn't given up on the idea of owning his own magazine. In early 1848 he began giving readings and lectures to raise money for that venture. He also began seeking the companionship of other women, but this was a strange and unstable effort. In his many letters he made declarations of love to several women at the same time—literary or not, married or not, it didn't seem to matter.

For a time he was engaged to Sarah Helen Whitman, a rich, middle-aged widow who was also a poet. This episode was a complete disaster. To convince her to marry him, he tried to kill himself by taking laudanum. She then agreed to marry him, but only if he would sign a prenuptial agreement and promise never to drink again. Poe promised, but it wasn't long before he resumed drinking.

Neither one of them was broken-hearted when the engagement was called off.

Poe was bothered by his reputation as an alcoholic. "I have absolutely no pleasure in the stimulants in which I sometimes so madly indulge," he once wrote. "It has not been in pursuit of pleasure that I have periled life and reputation and reason. It has been in the desperate attempt to escape from torturing memories, from a sense of insupportable loneliness, and a dread of some strange and impending doom."

In the summer of 1849 Poe went to Richmond, intent on raising funds for his magazine. It was a disturbing journey. Before he left, he got his papers in order and gave Maria Clemm instructions about what to do if he died. Then, while traveling, he suffered an attack of paranoia. Convinced that two men were trying to kill him, he got off the train in Philadelphia and sought refuge at the home of a friend. His friend made sure that no harm came to Poe while he was in this nervous state of mind. After two weeks Poe insisted on continuing his journey.

In Richmond, Poe renewed his acquaintance with his boyhood sweetheart, Sarah Elmira Royster, whose father had intercepted Poe's letters long ago. Sarah was now a widow, and Poe visited her often. He soon begged her to marry him, promising that he would be everything to her that she could desire. She suspected that Poe was interested not in her but in her money; nevertheless, they had come to a "partial understanding" when Poe left for a business trip to New York. He told her that he would return soon to Richmond. Almost in the same breath, however, he added that he had a feeling he would never see her again.

He was right.

On October 3, 1849, Edgar Allan Poe was found in Baltimore —unconscious, dirty, and dressed in clothes that were not his own. No one knows for sure what happened to him, but there is a possible explanation. It was election day in Baltimore, and since Poe was found near a polling place, it was widely thought that he had been drugged with alcohol or opiates and forced to vote over and over again in various polling places in the city. This practice, in which the victims were usually foreigners or strangers to the city, was called "cooping." It was fairly common at the time.

Poe was taken to Washington College Hospital, where he regained partial consciousness the next day. Trembling, pale, and drenched in perspiration, he ranted and raved to "spectral and

imaginary objects on the walls.''
He was calmer on the following
day, but he was never able to tell
his doctor what had happened to
him. And when his doctor asked
him if he would like to see his
friends, Poe responded with sud-
den, bitter energy.
"Friends!" he exclaimed.
"Friends! My best friend would
be he who would take a pistol and
blow out these damned wretched
brains!"
Shortly after this outburst, Poe
entered a state of violent delirium,

calling out the name "Reynolds" and fighting the nurses who tried to keep him in bed. This continued for a day or so, until exhaustion took over.

In a letter to Maria Clemm, his doctor recounted the end:

"Having become enfeebled from exertion, he became quiet, and seemed to rest for a short time; then, gently moving his head, he said, *'Lord help my poor soul!'* and expired."

It was October 7, 1849, and Edgar Allan Poe was finally at rest.

$\mathcal{W}$e wish to thank:

Adrien Delessert, Dorothy Johnson, John Mucci,

Virginia Simonin, and Taylor Simonin

The Northeast Audubon Center, Sharon, Connecticut

The Berkshire School, Sheffield, Massachusetts

The Emma Willard School, Troy, New York

The West Point Museum, United States Military

Academy, West Point, New York

Printed in Italy